SEE ME IMPROVING

TRAVIS NICHOLS

SEE ME IMPROVING

COPPER CANYON PRESS
PORT TOWNSEND, WASHINGTON

Cover art: Whiting Tennis, *Study for Nomad*, 2008. Spray paint on card-board, 11 × 7 inches. Courtesy of the artist and Greg Kucera Gallery.

Many thanks to the editors of the following publications, where versions of these poems first appeared:

aPlod, Baffling Combustions, Boston Review, Both, Can We Have Our Ball Back?, Crowd, GlitterPony, Isn't It Romantic?, and *State of the Union.*

The author would also like to thank Eric Baus, Joshua Beckman, Monica Fambrough, Peter Gizzi, Noah Eli Gordon, Brian Henry, Noy Holland, Paul Killebrew, Laura Solomon, Michael Wiegers, and Matthew Zapruder for their support.

Copper Canyon Press is in residence at Fort Worden State Park in Port Townsend, Washington, under the auspices of Centrum. Centrum is a gathering place for artists and creative thinkers from around the world, students of all ages and backgrounds, and audiences seeking extraordinary cultural enrichment.

LIBRARY OF CONGRESS CATALOGING-IN-PUBLICATION DATA
Nichols, Travis, 1979–
  See me improving / Travis Nichols.
    p. cm.
  ISBN 978-1-55659-312-3 (pbk. : alk. paper)
  I. Title.

PS3614.I3532S44 2010
811'.6—dc22

2010021882

98765432 FIRST PRINTING

COPPER CANYON PRESS
Post Office Box 271
Port Townsend, Washington 98368
www.coppercanyonpress.org

CONTENTS

SEE ME IMPROVING

Florida

When I was a kid my dad told me
the stars made the sounds of crickets.
The silver trills that had kept me up until
then every night weren't spilling from
the legs of little black insects but from brilliant
points of light in the sky.
He said this to me from outside my window
in the early morning or deep night in a sleep voice
I thought was the Gulf of Mexico
fumbling into the shore, so I whispered back,
The ocean was a liar, and I knew it because the other day
my dad told me the stars weren't spider eggs but
distant silent suns so far away they may already have died
and only the light exists of them now
in the great invisible net cast out by our eyes.
Then something strange happened.
His giant bald head rose into the window frame followed
by his one green eye, one blue eye, then his red-
veined nose and finally his beard-fuzzed mouth
which sang out in a clear human voice
I have been afraid of ever since.

The Empirical Field

Why is it so lovely to come inside someone, Bernadette?
I ask you because you understand the loveliness of having someone
come inside you, which seems to me the scary end
of twins in struggle, until at last you wrest my becoming
from me and want to quiver and talk about moaning
while I am the absence of clouds. Not the same
to bleed inside someone's hands or speak into her mouth
or press our ears together. There is magic in coming,
though there seems to be magic in sneezing, too,
kissing, though it too can be drowned in terror.
When Kiley's elbow touched my elbow my heart became erect,
and once when Anna and I kissed it felt like we were passing
an owl pellet back and forth with our tongues,
but I kissed Monica at Pont Neuf until the world turned red.
I kissed your book, Bernadette, but it is not the same.
Here in the library the fire alarm just barged in my ear
and the terror that shot through me was like coming.
There was an earthquake here yesterday morning and I barely felt
anything. This morning I woke up at 8 a.m. and really believed
it was 8 p.m. and I had slept through the whole day,
which would have been what I'd imagine it feels like
when you're a woman and you've come around someone. Bernadette,
if you were a man I would let you be horrible to me.
If I were a woman like you I'd ring out through the library
until all the boys had come inside me.

Elegy

Last night I dreamt I danced with Jimmy Schuyler.
Orange clouds piled in a black sky
and his voice spun blue and yellow around my neck.
"My dreams drift well past dancing," he said
as we left off swaying. My ear upturned.
"Open your mouth," he said. "Stop breathing.
Let stillness sit with sadness awhile."

The moon hung in a silver sack out there,
far away from our strings and snares.
"Bye now," he said. "Remember, that if you breathe,
our music will be swept inside of you forever.
Don't be evil, son. Bye now."

I wish I had been another creature
and had never once moved,
only let my stringy heart be still
and borne by a skylit bulb into the quiet.
But I breathed once, shook and cried.
As the music kept on I looked out the window,
over no one's shoulder.

Wild Is the Wind

There is a movie called *She's Gotta Have It*.
There is a blizzard in Massachusetts today.
Twenty-one people died in Chicago last night.
Two of my friends live there,
but I have never wanted to live there
because it is cold there and people die
from the cold and the wind and from each other.
There is a movie called *Chicago*.
I saw it yesterday in Massachusetts.
The wind is shaking our house this morning
but it's warm inside. One of my friends
in Chicago loves to have sex, the other
thinks she might but she's scared
because she passed out the first time
she had sex with someone else but that
was only a few months ago before it got so cold
in Chicago. I've had sex with one of my friends from Chicago
but not the other one though I wouldn't have sex
with either of them now after I've read how it is always
colder in Chicago than it is in Massachusetts
because of the wind. "Wild Is the Wind" is a song
by Nina Simone about not having sex with your friends
in Chicago. That's not true. Twenty-one people
died in Chicago last night but not two of my friends
or me because I live in Massachusetts.

Conscientious Objector

Caution and doubt are dreams of the dead.
The mountain doesn't move.
I split the raspberry with my tongue,
tear the strawberry with my teeth.
Mammals arch their backs
to break the surface of the Sound.
Ancient weapons turn to soil,
tools, too. Hungry ghosts strip and poison,
pigs aerate. A Dall's porpoise
conquers the water.
I crawl through ancient tubes
with the earth in my ear.
My family dies for the flag,
the one in Jasper Johns's painting,
on your beach towel.

*

A square inch of pleasure
equals a square inch of pain.
Arrive with a chill. Leave with a fever.
Dream through pools of sweat.
That actor—he never opens his eyes!
Drift away into the succulent charms of the sick.
Those thoughts that can only happen there
and no one has yet brought any back for good.
We've all been to that dark space.
What quiet deal did you make?
Healed, should I climb a tree? Get a head cold?
I step out for the first time in weeks
into all this painful sprouting.

*

Cats that go out
die, so our cat stays
in. Boo Radley.
He will die, too.
I pass my hand
through his fur and feel
his breath. Here,
I wish I could write the words
from which you could learn
what I so much would like to know.

*

On the bus
I text my friends:
"Drunk!"
No one writes back.
The bus ride is long.
I am drunk and it is not cute.
I am old. I go home.
Sleep it off.

*

There are no rules here
but those I dream up.
Take this work.
Is it clear?
Do you feel dumb?
I do.
That is the point.
(That is the point.)
Let's feel this point
rip us from the world.
Let's float free
in the new air.
You and me   dummy.

*

The sun does not fall
from the sky,
but to watch it set
and think so
is a trick.
If you say it,
someone will see it.
The sun falls.
He runs for home
with eyes shut tight
for fear of the crash.
He will wait
for the sick burn
from the shard of sun
to hit his neck flesh
as his eye melts
in a hot gush
down his cheek.

*

That art leads to war
there is no doubt.
That war leads back
is true, too.
That oil is cash,
that kids die,
that blood flows in downy streaks,
it is all true.
That we know what we know
when we do what we do,
there is no doubt.

*

Let's learn!
The bird is brown.
Its beak is hooked.
Its tail goes up.
Its body hops.
The bird is a wren.
It flies past my eyes.
I breathe in and out.
I write it down.

Testimonial

All my life I've felt destined
not for the greatness of my heroes
but the goodness of their followers.
I knew, even when I found a piece
of tooth in my Sausage McMuffin,
I would surmount the poverty
and dullness of my youth.
I knew neither my poverty nor my youth
would be significant enough
to attract attention,
only simple enough
to graft onto the great biographies.
Even when I felt uncommon and angry enough
to steal balloons from the drugstore
and spit red paintballs through a peashooter
at people making out in the park I knew
I was no Billy the Kid.
Even now as I stare at the snow-covered sidewalk,
a mildly pleasant stupor trickles over my skull,
because I know my tracks
will lead straight and true to the library,
just as they trail behind me.
And I know this evening I will settle
down to watch *The Searchers* and I will see
a faint shimmer shoot from my forehead
to the window where it will rest a moment,
flare up in someone's passing headlights,
then fade back into simple reflection.

Youth Is Not Absolution for Treachery;
It Is a Morning Star of Some Kind

If you keep punching at a man's head
it will mix his mind. So fast.
So pretty.
I want my brain to be the jangled thud
my body makes when it bangs against the ground.
I want you to say my name,
knock a broken branch against its tree
and that song will be a page
in a book you love to hold in your hand
because it is a birdcall that proves
you are privy to a superhuman scale.
I believe God is healing my soul right now
by killing my body. Slowly.
The opposite is true for your body, illuminated
by a light fired from another world,
seeing what other men have only thought.
Infinite are the fast mercies,
infinite the pretty occlusions.

Don't Worry Me

The Lord shined
a light on
my weary soul
when I was
in Bruegger's Bagels.
It's a tawdry
world, my friend
and the angles
don't match up,
but the Lord
shined a light
on my soul
and I have no idea
what it means.

I'm all hunted
down.
Hunted down
like a swan
in a briar patch
wearing a leather hat.

Ain't nobody clean.
Listen here:
Ain't nobody
clean.
I seen a chicken
lay a rotten egg.

I seen a angel
moan and whine.
I tell it
with my eyes.

It happens fast.
The bottle is out
tonight. No one
wants it. The court
won't hear it.
The dogwood and I
go dancing
under its branches,
but no one
hears the music
of our stuttered souls.
No one
is a optimist.

Everything is torture
but slow and dull.
Mysteries and gospels
keep me through.
This is no different.
Can you find God?
He's hunting you
with a pencil.

The Hand

Everything is true, dig.
If I feel a sad plop in my soul
when my friends hang out with other friends
while I stay home to work on the sad plop opus
and the first real spring evens outside,
am I codependent or just some other
nameless kind of loser?
It isn't ironic anymore, our truth is
simply this pathetic and I guess
newly sincere according to the attorney general
who is clearly still our enemy,
right?
I lost my fat little notebook the other day,
so now all those half-unwritten poems
belong to me only in my mind
and belong to you,
only in your surreptitious daydreams of me.
The sun shines where my friends are.
Here where I am asleep on my sweatshirt
my face fills with lines.
Animated by a hand,
I am a small blue sock from Ohio.

New England

When my scalp retreats
to the back of my skull
and my intestine fires flare
through their tubes, I know
I am beginning. When the skin
on my back begins to itch,
when my nose hairs freeze up,
when the ulcers in my mouth
pulse and my eyeballs dry out, then
I know I am beginning to bloom.
"Ding Dong!"
I yell, "Ding Dong!" and the sky bursts
open like a boil and a branch flies
from my mouth and plunges into a cloud,
rooting around there until it cradles
sunlight then pulls it back
into my belly with a whoomp.
You know how it is.

A Poem from Bled

Secondhand smoke after a day of sunshine and my hand
is lathered in tight lotion just like when I was a baby
and my brains were dashed on the hot asphalt.
I couldn't stay in my yellow safety seat.
A flat breast slides down the mountain into the lake,
and we bake cookies on the stones.
Can you feel the day
tightening a crystal vice around your perverted sensibility?
No one understands this kind of life,
but it is mine
and I refuse to hang myself
with ropes of dried ostrich blood
just so the illusion of ease may prevail
over every greasy bedpost.
Take off, greasy bedpost!
Fly into the first morning clouds
to be cleansed by their movement!
The hay dries on the rack.
The beekeeper paints his little doors.
The skin of even the mountain goat
tightens in the evening air,
so paddle with vacuous cheer
into your fat bottle of pink soda and I will plunge
into some sunny buttocks with the grace of God's eraser.

Disappearing Song of the Distracted Mind

A poem needs a reader—
    how will I seduce you?—
Never been so good at it, usually
    just hang around until
        someone decides, "Quiet
dude in the corner's not so bad," then
    BOOM!

A nice little story.
How about—you still there?—
a pinched penny forehead?
    Lacquered Lautréamont Huaraches?

A good friend walks in
humming the same song,
    filling a glass with ice,
        making a grocery list,
            sipping a fizzy drink.

(Class resentment seeps from the syllables.
    Get with the program!
Stop giggling! What is the secret?)

The search is on
    for a pen. Will it continue
        into this room
            of anxious striving?

Dear, dear reader.

      Everyone has advice for you.

      Perpetual misunderstanding blocks your clear mind.

             What is a mind, even?

Nexus of silent, simultaneous language that every once in a while forms a distinct phrase, then applauds itself?

And so many minds drifting through the city in their cranium carriages, sending impulses to communicate—"let me out out out!"—mistranslated into "walk to work," "let loose stream of babble," "listen to stream of babble," "be calmed by deciphering printed matter," "just keep turning the pages, you carcass, and I won't shudder and spaz—oops!—too late!"

Grabby kumquat.   Will the mariners beat the angels today?

First Light at Lascaux

Behind my hand is another hand.
Behind my head, another head.
Iron filings fill the hand,
sway with the movements of the head.
A mouth made of aluminum moths
moves in the mouth of the head.
Blue ink flows from the veins in the hand,
tooth-wounds open in the ears of the head.
Blight hands move inside the hand,
shaded from the light behind the head.

Behind my hand lamplit babies run through the forest,
lightning all around above and behind them.
The civil war rages over their sky-brightened eyes
but they are fleshy and pink, pink and fleshy and they
will win the wind from the wind.
Engendered of light, treacle-headed, bellied.
Leaf rustle. Morning light. Descent.
The forests stay dark.
The crucifix lodged in my temple, the defection
flowing sub-sight, sub-vestments, sub-speech
will never topple my empire of twine,
trace the world on waxed paper,
float torn silvery wings from a queen ant
into the fertile crescent,
over my palm,
to where my forest photos grow untended.

Behind my head my daughter sleeps in a lute-string hut.
Her mother dead from the purge,
I fly in the branches of imaginary trees.
An elegiac lake laps against our boathouse.
I'm flying in the gum from the superwhite body.
In the lake, in the sky. In my daughter:
the other white body,
supine under circle wound string.

Behind my hand the white body bats its blue-veined wings,
prunes the sea-trees under a blue sky.
Between the green sea and the blue sky
fishermen float Viennese fish songs.
The white body pulls the branches to it
and sings of marlin fish swallowing stars midleap.
Behind my head breath fills the air,
steel bowls fall onto the snow plic
ploc a child no bigger than small change
calls from her window j'ai faim.
The neighbors wheel wine and bread to her
on a scalped red scarf pulley
above their green grass communal square.
Behind my head, a hand.
Behind my hand, the bluet sky.

Blue Prince of Breath

She is a series of small movements.
Two unparallel shadows on the stair.
The soft yellows strike the walls around her,
swell and cast bells through the tubes between us.
Such an emergency presupposes a world,
ugly and unlike a dream,
where I am everyone.
I look at her as if she were paint.
She looks at me as if I were felt.
My heart, snug and dry in her underwear,
opens an idea behind me,
a foreign syntax betwixt her boots and overcoat.
The idea of her legs over the next.
One over the other.

On the 730th Day God Made Me Happy

I dreamt we fell in love.
You bought new sheets for the bed
and made dinner from breadcrumbs
and yellow squash. The red-fringed ivy bobbed
as the wind touched it,
stirring the building to feel.

This was before our descent
into winter, when I believed
the world would freeze me
for secretly believing I could be satisfied
forever without fiery ropes
dredging my shoulders nightly.

Our outsides are cold this morning,
slid upon by foreign sheets.

It will rain tonight and tomorrow, so this
morning we should wake. It will rain,
but we should drive through it,
wrapped in buzzard wings.
Because it is fall something will die
and fall. Something already died.
Its falling ghost guides these wings
flying over our rising bodies as we sleep.

When we fall into wakefulness we hear something
faintly flapping away. Clearly it was nothing
but a revenant sound from the dream world's ear, from

inside, and it can never escape outside, though I do hear
something—winter is coming again, but we will live
through it wrapped in each other's paper wings.

Unwrapped and awake I crouched
in green, snow-filled serpentines,
awaiting some deranged purity to alight
on my white raincoat, but all I fell into
was sleep again and then
further. The walls felt portentously close.
I shuffled to where they were closer,
but my face grew colder.

In an avalanche getting naked only helps
if there is another body next to yours. Alone,
all you can hope for is a dog with a barrel
around its neck to stumble into your blue-shadowed bank,
fallen from the sky like a flake. The earth turns
under you until you hit it
and turn too.

It has been five centuries since our dreamgirl drowned
in the book, five thousand years since God
drowned the world, but only a few hours since you
dredged me from a dream
with only the sound of your breath.
Even side by side we are still separated,
our bodies surrounded, I think and sigh, but then your eyes
unfold and wordlessly it seems we've had the same dream.

Your eyelashes run with spectral dew.
I don't know why or how your voice has fallen
into my breath, so now even when you sleep I am wed.
Gentle enough to be angry and angry enough to hold my breath
until our patch of earth turns away from the sun. The sky
presses close, bruised by the parting, but soon it will lighten,
and our world will drink coffee and stretch in the sunlight to begin
work on the yellow and blue task until more hibiscus bloom
on the horizon, only to billow out into the blue
for a brief moment then fall into winter again,
but I will wake next to you
naked in the snow and breathing.

Aim High

Leave home
and hope
home leaves you
for an hour at least.
A pill could make it,
not you, turn black
and die. Right? Take it.
Kiss me on the mouth.
Shut me up.

Gallant Phantoms through the Pineapple Door

World in a sling slung over the tops of jars
whizzing into forgotten triangles.

A slow return to breathing.

All the all filtering top to middle, poured
down to mix with the sediment in the walls.

Limes cut by a hacksaw,
clotted cream thrown into the fan.

No one calls the fire department.
No one calls the police.

A vacation spot in the material world.
The happiness experiment, so called.

Dirt under the fingernails,
fatigue lifting off shoulders.

Off she goes to untangle her necklaces.
Light shed in blasts not bleats.

Uncommon arrangements winnowed to slivers
understood only as they pinion fingertips,
pushing blood in bubbles up to round the surface.

Open a vein, an artery, a heart.
Let the air in.

Let's spend some lives together.

We can make a nest in palimpspastic branches and puffs,
over there by the old house, the hair smell, and the music.

I Feel Right at Home in This Faraway City

"He is the strangest stranger," they say,
"and he is your stepdad."
From the new hole in my back,
a bloody mist swirls up each morning.
I say, "Let's all enjoy this doughnut
despite the triangular penetration of ravens
into our fragile and fat day."

The New Privacy

Heart full of helium,
tongue full of copper,
I ask if you are all right—"Are you
okay?"—until you can be nothing
but not all right, not okay.
Together then we are
hysterical, but now you seem
more hysterical than me because
this weird deer wants in
to sleep between us
on the bed. Listen weird deer:
Even if you try to gore me with
your four icy antlers I will fall asleep
to the sound of my lady's heart
beating in my forehead
not your bloody hooves falling
into her mouth.

Effusion for Eleanor

Yellow jackets pose in front of the votives.
A white mountain opens itself for the mouse.
I write this poem on a paper towel with a cheap pen
as my sister once wrote to me on a paper bag:
"On the snow: blue ink covered with snow.
Ceramic deer heads mounted on blue suede."
I'm shaking from something other than the cold,
the laugh of the tribe or my elders' weak intestines.
Even Anselm will one day die,
from the belly if I had to guess,
and one thousand cigarettes will fall
from the mouths of one thousand schoolchildren.

Thanks, Kids

Paul's brother got his girlfriend pregnant,
but young people are no longer
able to sustain utopian visions.
Why is my belt buckle so hot?
It has to be her decision.
Dread has heated my belt buckle.
An infectious airborne virus
has drifted from Hong Kong to
Germany, and it isn't hopeful
or dreadful, but it might be influenza
or maybe global bioterrorism.
I'm putting an alert icon
at the end of this poem that
will remain there until the threat
has diminished. Look!
Some kids are having a snowball fight!
One winds up and hurls a well-packed
beaner right into the chest of another.
This other kid stumbles a little.
Seems to be stunned. No, she's waiting
for the hurler to turn around—clever kid!
Now the hurler has turned around
and the clever girl is lobbing a loose bit of snow
underhand. It splashes lightly across
the hurler's snow-panted fanny! What fun!
Now the clever girl is on the move,
running and laughing hysterically!

Lament for Scott Street

The sun slides under our feet at midnight
though my soles have never flashed
with anything but aching.
A poet is dead, Louisa says.
His heart seized last night as he walked home
from a party. He had a full life
and I'm sure he clutched after all of it
as it fled from him in verse.
They're all dying, Travis.
Where his books were last week,
this morning there isn't even dust.
Just yesterday you walked in here
as if the poems were nothing but a dream.
Today, you've got some wild turtle on a leash.

A Banjo and a Bicycle

The joy of falling
obliterated by impact.
Time condensed to a foam
only industry abides.
The cat engulfed by a nightmare,
converting sunlight into something darker,
that ancestral dementia
talked over since childhood.
The flowers blossom into flames. Listen:
There will never be enough.
Even if you cry from your pointillist breast
a legacy of hot bruises
all the major keys
in your minor works
will fall to the floor and scatter.
All the money is gone.

The Work

You scrape your tooth
on a tin can
and it is plain.
The creased line
the sun finds.
There is joy
in not knowing.
School is out.
A blue tarp
fills the sky.
It falls on the wet grass.
A kid's game.
The sun is out.
The blue tarp falls.
There is no code.
It is plain.

See Me Improving 1

All the straight men and lesbians in my town
are buying roses this morning
but not for each other. We huddle
in my room hoping either a straight man
or a lesbian will turn our heat back on,
so this afternoon there will be a difference
when we go from the indoors to the outdoors,
where I will buy orange roses for you,
and you will buy an orange book for me,
and this evening we will leave them both
in the cold house with the furry cat,
so we can have a code orange night.

See Me Improving II

This morning someone's mediocre mind
crumbled into my coffee
and all day since, the prodigal have carved history
with knives pulled from their wounds.
All my precious feelings
have floated away inglorious enough
to not even ripple the air on their way out.
A light rain fills the windows.
The night I see so little of begins
applauding performance.
The cat stretches on the rug.
The leeks bend and sweeten in the saucepan.
I stir them.

See Me Improving III

These kids are always screaming
and I can't think if I ever screamed
so loud about anything except
when I screamed "soccer
is for faggots" in middle school.
I don't think I've screamed since, surely
was never so disingenuous in screaming,
soccer being my favorite sport, faggots
my best friends, chicken-legged tomboys screaming
apple juice and earrings every recess just foils.
Duangchung Thongsouk (later Cindy)
screamed when we wouldn't let her
play Smear the Queer and Brian screamed
when she flashed her vagina from pink sweatpants,
because, he said to the principal (screaming),
it was "veiny."

See Me Improving IV

My hymnal once held a more perfect hymn.
Sean is in my coat sleeves.
Someone else underneath my hands is coming.
My friend Carolyn is in a band called Lovers.
If there is a heaven I want to go.
Monica tills snake-handling fields.
The love song is about me.
It's New Year's Eve and it feels like this
to be alive and have friends inside you.
Trees are bleeding into the sky, Paul,
with your tongue in my teeth singing.
After she sings she looks at me.
I love everyone and you.

See Me Improving V

Breathing but true
breath never comes
on Sunday afternoons
in spring when even
the acorns wear pink.
Who could breathe?
Only wake up to another
miserable morning of tedious rain
and responsibility.
Have you seen our cat?
We forgot to tell our parents.
Why did we huff
dust remover? Because
we weren't afraid.

See Me Improving VI

Tomorrow in a kindergarten of trees
a carrot will spurt
from a small hole in the ground
and pin the berserk heart
of a rabbit to the sun.

See Me Improving VII

Soon it will be spring!
There—half a garbage can lid
has risen out of the snow
like a shallow corpse after
a flood! Soon I will find
the pen I lost in the driveway,
drink a beer and smoke two cigarettes.
A chunk of ice just
fell by my foot.
The squirrels run up the trees.
They don't want another
snow-watching party until
next year when the phone will
ring and I will say hello yes hello?

See Me Improving VIII

I don't know
what that means.
Conscripts blare.
So what?
Fallujah doesn't care
what my prima donna
man in a box
does with his day.
"Lawnmower jockey rides again,"
says the pigeon.
Ordinary feelings.
I never meant to scoff.
Relentless.
I should have been
relentless.

See Me Improving IX

What do I have in my yard tonight?
I have a possum and a raccoon,
a kitten and a squirrel—no,
not a squirrel because it is nighttime.
Now I have a skunk and a bear.
A bear? Yep. And another bear.
Two black bears by the fence.

See Me Improving X

On this first prepubescent spring afternoon
skateboard wheels shave the road's throat,
the brown and gray ice runs into puddles,
ducks splash by the crew, and the people
are ecstatic—winter is over and the war
is not yet here! I don't care
about your airborne viruses
or Snapple warriors, America, the world melts away
and leaves nothing of itself behind
except a steady sound unlike any other so
I'm going to spit off this bridge like I'm free,
without consequence.

Morning Song

A crushed crimper in the gravel. A secession.
Imprints on a page. I pass my mind over
the things of this world as a man passes a stick,
thinking it a wand, or a squeegee,
thinking it could clean or fundamentally alter
the composition of a thing
rather than simply and privately acknowledge its puny
existence. A hoodie. A jogger. Two white girls.
A stray hair. Undone and unfinished. The seagulls.
The ravens. The immature hawk on the fence sliding down
into the bushes where the little sparrows are.
The little sparrows. The immature hawk. The orange juice
and bread I'm going to buy for breakfast.

Insurgent

White men preen and spit-polish their spears.
The war has passed them by.
I roam free in the dirt with the law in my teeth,
a widower in search of a widow,
a golden ode in my ear bulging against my brain,
a swollen bulb with a piercing root.
This blade rests in my rib
bleeding flecks of rust into my fatty slabs.
Snuff out the candle and I will rise with the smoke
into the incarnate wind.
Is it black? Only against open eyes.
Beyond eyes I see into a darkness. Another breath.
Words. Music. An echoing gorge under a meat red sky.
The bone in my throat is buzzing.

The Facts of Spring

A ghostface hawk flapped its wings once,
guiding its spiral by instinct or mind,
each unlike the red impatiens pushing up
through the rocks in the yard and the wake
that will be carved by our days through the weather.
Here is a toast to the hurt that holds and guides you—
bassoony geese honking overhead. As our hearts honk,
they move through our strung-out cult of hucksters,
plucked and plucked again by the invisible hand
until cultures emerge and only a chocolate church
remains beside the violent autumnal death scenes.
To your left a Japanese ghost merchant and a knave lie
on Limerick Road in a dirty house littered
with giant insect traps and inverted speakers
moving into themselves in mono, unlocking nucleotides
to rearrange again when the cultures call for them.
When the rain falls like coins into the sea that baby
won't mind if the brine-held sins of the father are
public record, but my son will—sailor by blood not relation,
thin as the skin of the ocean.

Smile

The calm position of my wind-chapped face
after a day outside and a night of bloody noses.
It feels so cinematic. Behind it I picture
myself as I would like to be seen—
empty of all self-regard, -importance, -loathing—
but my teeth yellow as they recede
away from spectators into my mouth.
Only good friends and a few lovers know.
Everyone else regards two shiny fronts and a crinkled smile.
Charming. "Always home on time for dinner."
"No more midnight drives into the mountains on acid."
"No more vain attempts to live outside the jurisdiction."
A human sees itself unexpectedly reflected,
brushing the teeth, suddenly ordinary, ugly, ready to die.

Recess

Once when I was small a great big granddaughter came up to
me and said how do you do? I am illegitimate & dumb what's
your name? Test scores show me to be in the bottom of my
class should we be friends? Sure I said why not you only have
one time on this carousel of grotesquely defined bumblebees &
juice is an elixir want some? No she said I want proof. What's
your name? Long before last Christmas I said I sought a ham-
mer to shape my name but I hurt my elbow see? The sunlight is
on my mind she said so I don't believe it. C'mon I said I cared
for you inside my head when we played Follow the Leader—
When the leader said snap she said you snapped two times!
That shut me up. Lay me down in a bed of brown rice and re-
turn on occasion to doubt she said. Layer my surface with mus-
tard greens & call an ambulance. I can't keep up I lied but it
was too dark for secrets & two mewling associates had taken
her away from the gates by then.

March 21, 2003

A song is words and music.
Poetry is an ovary with an eyeball in it.
My life is a machine
producing words
meant to form a chairlift
moving slow enough to never reach
the top of a mountain no one
has ever seen. Will the sound
of my stocking feet sliding
down the wall ever seem joyous
without marijuana?
Yep.
I want to rest forever
in the moment when my mind sucks
down a new draft of knowing.
Only then will I never again
be obliged
to use the bathroom,
but I'm not there yet
because even now I can feel
my bladder filling,
waiting down there to sound
the alarm when I least expect it.

Vita Nuova

Sun face.   Moon face.
Is it okay to ignore what's in between?
The camellia blossoms brown and fall
onto the skeleton leaves held up by grasses and moss.
When I dance I will raise the dead.
Private inhale.   Public exhale.
The false face dichotomy cresting into the juice of thought,
the slow movement of rain on the sidewalk.

Undone, the dead happen now
only within the air,
trapped inside the air in the blood.
Sun face.   Moon face.
At what moment was she alive
in the face and ha-ha grounded for life
and at what moment
dead? In her face.

Over the tops of trees, brothers,
my brains will fly.
Suicide always a gun, a flash
filling the eyes from below.
Corporeal but sublimely abstract
to die lit up by an echoing.
Babies. My Baby. Her sun face. Some flower,
as we walk in the Rhododendron Glen,
scented like chocolate. All ages
commensurate with killing.
A shoveler and his mate

dance underwater while the coots
and teals look on.
And us.

On 19th you can watch
the sun rise over the mountains,
over a house made to echo the sun.
When the cold shotgun barrel presses
it's okay to be afraid
of the worms,
of never being the young one
in the worms.

This is our camellia.
To be shot in the face.
This is our generational starburst on the arm,
in the eyes. When I go
I want to be smiling,
she says, daring the bullets
to raise their moon faces
to the dead of night.

In the sunlight we see two
bald eagles chasing each other,
swooping over the houses,
coming together and plunging past the tree line,
over the house where it happened.
At the grocery store: photos.
The clerks crying. I can see the flash of the gun
through the blinds.
Last night on the porch, a moose.

A mountain. A pickup truck.
A hollow feeling below a schism.
Twins.
Your body is still warm when I sleep
because your blood
still flows
through my dreams.

Eulogy for What Will Take Care of You

Would you rather be a bird or a ghost?
Both bear the delicate flame out of itself
into ash gratuitously, but everything comes
to the bird as everything
but tedious survival comes to everyone
but you whom it comes to
gracefully.

I have ten words on my fingers.
None of them will keep
your blood moving continuously
as a circuit run on field recordings of fields
and recordings of rolls and rolls
of magnetic tape rolling into one
part filament two parts night,
but only where it's torn. Can you see it?
There, where the white
turns yellow?
You could say the filament
is only a piece of the night
you can't go into,
but wouldn't you rather say
what you mean to say,
that waking up
never means
what it seems to mean?

Some of these frequencies
make scar tissue

if you let them cut through you
cleanly enough,
but no one talks about scars
the way he talks about tattoos,
though scars are more
familiar signs
that family means
what you can make
with what will take care of you.

Be patient.
The divine is always still and undone,
so be still and undo
in the unscarred morning
when the feathered pen showers sparks,
and your mind goes,
and your mouth dribbles after it.

The fluid is little things
moving together
like the blue
in a jellyfish.

Tonight, I am in a bar
because the rest of the city
is closed. My favorite voice
is lying here, in my mind,
wholly impersonal,
undivided and closer to my heart
than all of last year.

If I too used to like to
make out with make-believe girls,
then the saddest thing about them
is their inspiration didn't live long enough
to enjoy them,
as everyone in our interval
enjoys this beast hung by a hook.

Your skin is as beautiful
as anything through which
I've seen carried blood,
as real as the skin of everything
that can be forgiven,
which is everything
and everyone,
though this forgiveness means
what will take care of you
is never by itself alone but must live
side by side with its enemy.

We could have caught the boat together,
but we would have been broken
by its schedule,
because the boat and I
keep time differently,
though both the boat and I
could still bear
a more populous crossing
out of the terminal
on to the bay
and into the rain.

Could we salt the world
with our flavor?
Could we discover the gulls,
or feel our skins
as glorious organs of contour
and restraint? Or am I alone
on this boat propelled by voices?
It goes everywhere
as long as there is water
and a language
buoyed by water.

A voice is pulling you.
The boat is full.
The heart is empty.
The poems are all you can do
to keep from bearing out of this
and into that
with every pretty face.
Where your eye eyes what is
forever out of reach,
is knowing you would feel
horrible afterward any reason
not to feel good now? Yes.
And you love me for saying
yes.

War Hero

It's peaceful on the open roads,
veins splayed to the breeze.
I'm old-fashioned like that.
Black hat. Marble vine.
The snakes call you,
you come running.
A necklace of reflexes.

I do the same thing every day
and I'm a war hero,
curious to see what the day brings
but not curious enough
to change my routine.
I like that. It seems
small, but in pockets of verdure
it strikes out grand.

"Strength before honor." Before
breakfast we march.
What do I know?
In a nest rests an amber egg.
I sat on the seas
and could have named all the mammals,
but I was called to canvass
these inside areas instead.

Send me your tired, your weak,
your huddled masses.

I'm so sick of this shit,
        of being maligned by
withered saps with dusty hair.
        I surrender to the night's syndrome of quiet despair.
        I surrender to the weak home of longing poverty.
        I surrender to the Chinese deli and the Oxford shirt.

        I touch it and go peacefully
to die in combat,
        for the stages of grief
carry no water
        into the desert of no relation.

Something Touched My Heart

There was a time when songs were magic.
I've seen films of this time and when I catch myself
watching these films over and over I feel dead.
Rimbaud in front of the mirror buttering his hair
like he's Bob Dylan. All I want to do
is the dishes but here I am secretly singing
along, worrying about the rent and surrealism,
has it gone out of style? I believe
this life continues into that life
so looking forward to death holds no purpose,
but I do it anyway unsure of my purpose
or who relies on me for her purpose,
though someone surely does as I scribble on a wall,
kick over a trashcan, and dismiss people from my life
without so much as saying one word to them.
I apologize for falling from grace,
causing your embodied descent and forced
redemption, but that said I could use
another kind of salvation into
the headphoned world of song,
out of this one where I don't rightly love
those I love for fear of having to love
too long and again with the same love
when it changes. No one can help
lift the weight of the world so real,
and tumbling from the sky she goes
and now she knows she'll never be
afraid. Just because an action exists
in history doesn't mean we shouldn't do it.

So we're stoned what are you going to do,
tell us about the Beatles?
I don't believe in Beatles I only believe
love is nothing but a memento mori.
Move me to see my one holy life through two eyes.
The zinnia is so much more real today
than anyone with a mouth I think I'll slip
inside it and eat some tomatoes.

ABOUT THE AUTHOR

Travis Nichols was born and raised in Ames, Iowa. He lives in Chicago and is an editor at the Poetry Foundation. His writing has appeared in the *Believer*, the *Huffington Post*, *Paste*, the *Stranger*, and the *Village Voice*. His books include the poetry collection *Iowa* (Letter Machine Editions) and the novel *Off We Go Into the Wild Blue Yonder* (Coffee House Press).

The Chinese character for poetry is made up of two parts: "word" and "temple." It also serves as pressmark for Copper Canyon Press.

 Since 1972, Copper Canyon Press has fostered the work of emerging, established, and world-renowned poets for an expanding audience. The Press thrives with the generous patronage of readers, writers, booksellers, librarians, teachers, students, and funders—everyone who shares the belief that poetry is vital to language and living.

Copper Canyon Press gratefully acknowledges board member

JIM WICKWIRE

for his many years of service to poetry and independent publishing.

Lannan

NATIONAL
ENDOWMENT
FOR THE ARTS

WASHINGTON STATE
ARTS COMMISSION

Major support has been provided by:

Amazon.com

Anonymous

Beroz Ferrell & The Point, LLC

Golden Lasso, LLC

Gull Industries, Inc.
on behalf of William and Ruth True

Lannan Foundation

Rhoady and Jeanne Marie Lee

National Endowment for the Arts

Cynthia Lovelace Sears and Frank Buxton

Washington State Arts Commission

Charles and Barbara Wright

*To learn more about underwriting
Copper Canyon Press titles, please call
360-385-4925 x103*

Lannan Literary Selections

For two decades Lannan Foundation has supported the publication and distribution of exceptional literary works. Copper Canyon Press gratefully acknowledges their support.

LANNAN LITERARY SELECTIONS 2010

Stephen Dobyns, *Winter's Journey*

Travis Nichols, *See Me Improving*

James Richardson, *By the Numbers*

John Taggart, *Is Music: Selected Poems*

Jean Valentine, *Break the Glass*

RECENT LANNAN LITERARY SELECTIONS
FROM COPPER CANYON PRESS

Michael Dickman, *The End of the West*

James Galvin, *As Is*

David Huerta, *Before Saying Any of the Great Words: Selected Poems*, translated by Mark Schafer

Sarah Lindsay, *Twigs and Knucklebones*

Heather McHugh, *Upgraded to Serious*

W.S. Merwin, *Migration: New & Selected Poems*

Valzhyna Mort, *Factory of Tears*, translated by Franz Wright and Elizabeth Oehlkers Wright

Taha Muhammad Ali, *So What: New & Selected Poems, 1971–2005*, translated by Peter Cole, Yahya Hijazi, and Gabriel Levin

Lucia Perillo, *Inseminating the Elephant*

Ruth Stone, *In the Next Galaxy*

Connie Wanek, *On Speaking Terms*

C.D. Wright, *One Big Self: An Investigation*

For a complete list of Lannan Literary Selections from Copper Canyon Press, please visit Partners on our Web site:

www.coppercanyonpress.org

The poems are set in Janson, revived by Herman Zapf in 1937 from the original old-style serif typeface named for Dutch punchcutter and printer Anton Janson. The headings are set in Gill Sans Condensed, designed by Eric Gill. Book design and composition by Phil Kovacevich. Printed on archival-quality paper at McNaughton & Gunn, Inc.